The Credit Challenge Kit

Matthew McClain

For information contact: info@uptownmediaventures.com
Book and Cover design by Team Uptown

http://uptownmediaventures.com

ISBN: 978-1-68121-128-2

First Edition: December 2020

10 9 8 7 6 5 4 3 2 1

Dedicated to everyone who works hard and deserves another chance.

Table of Contents

Preface

This book gives the reader the process to make challenges to negative items on their credit report in a simple and informative fashion. The intent is to give the reader the necessary information to make such challenges right away, without excess verbiage, by giving step by step and concise instruction and direction.

Get Copies of Your Credit Report

Getting Credit Reports For Free

The three nationwide consumer reporting companies (Equifax, Experian and TransUnion) have set up one central service through which you can order your Free Annual Reports. You are eligible for one free credit report per year.

You're entitled to one <u>free copy of your credit report</u> every 12 months from each of the three nationwide credit reporting companies. Order online from annualcreditreport.com, the only authorized website for free credit reports, or call 1-877-322-8228. You will need to provide your name, address, social security number, and date of birth to verify your identity.

If you're not eligible for free reports, the cost to purchase one is up to $10, depending on your state. Or you can complete the Annual Credit Report Request below and mail it to:

Annual Credit Report Request Service
P.O. Box 105281
Atlanta, GA 30348-5281

Getting free credit reports is good, however, Free Annual Reports do not have scores. For that reason, it is recommend to spend $1 to get all 3 scores by signing up for credit monitoring.

Other Options to Obtain Credit Reports

AnnualCreditReport.com

This is a website through which you can order the free credit reports that you're entitled to by federal law. To make sure you're taking advantage of this right, you must order through AnnualCreditReport.com.

FreeCreditScore.com

Your credit score through FreeCreditScore.com can be acquired for free which is based on your **Experian** credit report. But to do so you must be enrolled in a trial subscription to a credit monitoring service. Failing to cancel within seven days will result in a monthly credit card charge.

myFICO.com

The only place you can get a free **FICO** score, the score most commonly used by lenders, is through myFICO.com. There's a catch, though. To get your free FICO score, you must sign up for a trial subscription to Score Watch, a credit score monitoring service.

If you don't cancel – you guessed it – your credit card will be charged.

CreditKarma.com

Here, you can get a free credit score without having to enter any credit card number. You don't have to enroll in a trial subscription and you don't have to cancel anything to avoid being charged. The score is your **TransUnion** credit score which is based on data from that credit report. An advantage this site offers is you can order an updated credit score through Credit Karma as often as you'd like, for free.

Quizzle.com

Quizzle gives you access to both your credit report and credit score – for free. There's no credit card required and you don't have to cancel a subscription to anything. They don't even need your social security number. Both the credit report and score are based on your data at **Experian**. You can get a free credit score and report from Quizzle twice a year.

Getting Reports and Scores Cheap with Credit Monitoring

Credit monitoring is a good choice because you can see the reports and scores as they change. Most credit monitoring companies charge $1 for a trial with instant access to all 3 reports and scores (a real bargain). Just be sure you're gaining access to all 3 reports and scores because some companies only give access to one.

You can cancel the free trial if ongoing credit monitoring is not wanted. But without credit monitoring there is no way to monitor the scores as they change, so it's recommended that you keep the monitoring service active for as long as you are repairing your credit.

Examine Your Reports Carefully

Nearly every consumer has an error on at least one credit report from one of the major credit bureaus, says Rhode. Credit bureaus generate your report on information they receive from your creditors; they don't verify.

Keeping your credit report a true reflection of you is very important. A person must carefully look for everything from typing errors, outdated and incomplete information to inaccurate account histories. You'll want to make a thorough list of items you dispute and why. Be dedicated and thorough.

If the negative information in your report is true, only time and improved habits can change that. Late payments, such as credit cards, and charged-off accounts remain on your report for seven years; bankruptcies for 10. Most creditors, however, look for a pattern of payment rather than focusing on one-time or rare occurrences; so consistent on-time bill payments will improve those blemishes.

Federal law requires the credit bureau to remove information that's incomplete, inaccurate, or unverifiable. For example:

• Your social security number (sometimes only the last four digits of your SSN appear on your credit report)

• Payments reported late that were actually paid on time

• Negative information that's passed the credit reporting time limit can be disputed for credit repair

• Accounts being reported by two collection agencies at once

• Accounts that don't belong to you

• Accounts reported as closed that are actually open

• Accounts discharged in bankruptcy that are reported delinquent or charged-off

The Challenge Process

Here are some guidelines for filing a credit dispute by mail:

1. Keep it simple. Include everything you need to, but stick to the facts using clear language.
   Now is not the time to trot out legalese or try to be fancy.
2. Send a separate dispute letter for each incorrect item rather than combining them.
3. Include copies of whatever evidence you have, whether it's a Social Security card showing your correct number, a canceled check showing a payment was made, bank statements, or anything that substantiates your claim.
4. To expedite things, send a copy of your dispute to both the credit bureau and the lender, collection agency, or whoever furnished them with the incorrect data.
5. Send your dispute by certified mail so you have proof it was received.
6. Use our credit dispute templates as a guide (see below).
7. Finally, don't give up! If your dispute is valid and the error continues to be reported by the credit bureaus, consider taking the case to an attorney. The Fair Credit Reporting Act was set up to protect you in these situations, and you do have legal recourse.
8. A credit dispute always starts with a Round 1 letter to a credit bureau. It never goes to a creditor.

Credit Reporting Agencies and Addresses

Challenge letters should be sent to all three major credit reporting agencies. The names and addresses are as follows:

Equifax Information Services LLC

P.O. Box 740241

Atlanta, GA 30374-0241

Phone: (800) 685-1111

Experian

P.O. Box 2104

Allen, TX 75013-0949

Phone: (888) 397-3742

TransUnion Consumer Solutions

P.O. Box 1000

Chester, PA 19022

Phone: (800) 916-8800

Sample Basic Dispute Letter

Here is a sample Round 1 dispute letter with sample dispute items. (Use only the challenges you need and delete the rest).

_____

[Date]

[Your Name]
[Your Address]
[City, State Zip]

[Your Date of Birth:]
[Social Security Number:]
[Credit Report Number:]

[Credit Bureau Name]
[Credit Bureau Address]
[City, State Zip]

Re: Letter to Remove Inaccurate Credit Information – Credit Report
#_____

To Whom It May Concern:

Matthew McClain

I received a copy of my credit report and found the following item(s) to have errors. See the attached copy of my credit report, where the errors have been highlighted.

Here, as follows, are items in error:

Incorrect Personal Information:

XXXXXXXXXXXXXXXX

Correct Personal Information:

XXXXXXXXXXXXX

The following accounts below are not mine:

Creditor's Name

Account Number

Explanation:

The account status is incorrect for the following accounts:

Creditor's Name

Account Number

Correct Status:

The following information is outdated (for example 7 years old). I would like it removed from my credit history report:

Creditor's Name

Account Number

Date of Last Activity

The following inquiries are more than two years old and I would like them removed:

Creditor's Name

Date of Inquiry

These inquiries below were not authorized:

Creditor's Name

Date of Inquiry

Explanation

The following accounts were closed by me and should state that:

Creditor's Name

Account Number

Other information I would like changed:

Explanation

The following accounts are more than seven years old and must be removed per statute.

Creditor's Name

Account Number

By the provisions of the Fair Credit Reporting Act, I demand that these items be investigated and removed from my report.

It is my understanding that you will recheck these items with the creditor who has posted them. Please remove any information that the creditor cannot verify.

I understand that under 15 U.S.C. Sec. 1681i (a), you must complete this reinvestigation within 30 days of receipt of this letter. Please send an updated copy of my credit report to the above address. According to the act, there shall be no charge for this updated report.

I also request that you please send notices of corrections to anyone who received my credit report in the past six months.
Thank you for your time and help in this matter.

Sincerely,

_____

[Signature]

_____
_____

(For best results, send this letter by some sort of verified mail. Include a copy of your government issued Photo ID (like your drivers license or passport) and proof of address (like a utility or insurance bill). Enclose a copy of the credit report containing the items you are disputing. It may also help to circle the items. Also include copies (not originals) of any paperwork you may have that validates your claims.)

The credit bureaus and creditors will send their replies directly to you. Credit bureaus have 30 days to conduct their investigation. (There are a few exceptions when this time frame may extend to 45 days, but 30 is the most typical.) This doesn't mean it will take the full 30 days before you receive a response, but this is the maximum time frame. This is a time when having written proof in the form of a receipt noting when the credit bureaus received your dispute may be helpful, so you know when the 30 days begins. You should receive notice informing you of the results from the credit bureaus within five business days after the investigation is completed.

If paper work or other evidence supports your claim, you should also send the dispute, with copies of the supporting information, to the banks, collection agencies or other providers.

Debt collection agencies can sometimes be aggressive in their collection tactics and trickier to deal with. Below is a sample letter, created by the Consumer Financial Protection Bureau, that you can send to a collection agency.

The purpose of this following letter is to make it clear that you do not owe a certain debt.

<u>Sample Letter to Debt Collection Agency</u>

[Date]

[Your name]
[Your return address]

[Debt collector name]
[Debt collector address]
Re: [Account number for the debt, if you have it]

Dear [Debt collector name],

I am responding to your contact about collecting a debt. You contacted me by **[phone/mail]**, on **[date]** and identified the debt as **[any information they gave you about the debt]**. I do not have any responsibility for the debt you're trying to collect.

If you have good reason to believe that I am responsible for this debt, mail me the documents that make you believe that. Stop all other communication with me and with this address, and record that I dispute having any obligation for this debt.

If you stop your collection of this debt, and forward or return it to another company, please indicate to them that it is disputed. If you report it to a credit bureau (or have already done so), also report that the debt is disputed.

Thank you for your cooperation.

Sincerely,

[Your name]

Some Subsequent Challenge Letters After Initial Denial

For each dispute letter you send, you will get a letter back that will explain what was removed (or not removed) and why. If there are further discrepancies a "Round 2" letter (or higher) disputes one (1) item and can be sent to the credit bureau or to the creditor/furnisher who is reporting the item.

Remember that the Credit bureaus have 30 days to conduct their investigation. If paper work or other evidence supports your claim, you should also send copies of the supporting information with your subsequent challenge.

Sample Subsequent Challenge Letter (Frivolous Letter Rejection)

[Date]

[Your Name]
[Your Address]
[City, State Zip]

[Your Date of Birth:]
[Social Security Number:]
[Credit Report Number:]

Matthew McClain

[Credit Bureau Name]
[Credit Bureau Address]
[City, State Zip]

RE: **FRIVOLOUS LETTER REJECTION**

To Whom It May Concern:

I am in receipt of your letter stating that my dispute of items in my credit report was "irrelevant and frivolous." I am upset that your credit reporting agency would try such a blatant stall tactic. I am demanding that you reinvestigate my credit file under the Fair Credit Reporting Act Section 611 [15 USC 1681I].

You have no way to ascertain the legitimacy of my action without investigating the items in question. Enclosed is a copy of my original letter and credit report with the disputed items highlighted. Additional stall tactics on the part of your organization will be reported to the Federal Trade Commission.

If you have any questions, please contact me at the address listed below. Thank you.

Sincerely,

[Your name]

Sample Subsequent Challenge Letter (Failure to Respond)

[Date]

[Your Name]

[Your Address]

[City, State Zip]

[Your Date of Birth:]

[Social Security Number:]

[Credit Report Number:]

[Credit Bureau Name]

[Credit Bureau Address]

[City, State Zip]

RE: **FAILURE TO RESPOND TO DELTETION/CORRECTION**

To Whom It May Concern:

On [insert date of first letter], I sent a letter requesting that you reinvestigate or delete disputed items from my credit report as well as place temporarily remove these items from my report during the investigation period. As of this date, you have failed to respond to my request. A copy of my original letter is attached for your review.

Matthew McClain

The law stipulates that you must investigate within 30 days of receiving my letter and respond within 5 days of completing your investigation. You have not followed the stipulations of the law.

I may suffer damages because I need to rely on an accurate and complete statement of my credit record and demand that you remove the disputed items from my report immediately as you failed to comply with the law.

Otherwise, I will contact the Federal Trade Commission and advise them of your apparent disregard for consumer protection laws. If you have any questions or need additional information, please contact me at the address noted below.

Sincerely,

[Your name]

Online Credit Challenges

In addition to sending a letter, you can also dispute online. It's recommend that you do both. Below are the websites where you can dispute:

Equifax

Online: www.ai.equifax.com/CreditInvestigation

Experian

Online: www.experian.com/disputes/main.html

TransUnion

Online: www.transunion.com/personal-credit/credit-disputes-alerts -reezes.page

About the Author

Mathew McClain, J.D., is an experienced financial planner and business lawyer with over 20 years of experience in portfolio investment and asset protection. He has assisted over a thousand clients in protecting their assets by the use of many varied legal mechanisms.

The Credit Challenge Kit

Matthew McClain

UP**TOWN**

MEDIA JOINT VENTURES
PUBLISHING

www.ingramcontent.com/pod-product-compliance
Lightning Source LLC
Chambersburg PA
CBHW051430200326
41520CB00023B/7422